※ **Enriching Faith** ※

LESSONS, PRAYERS AND ACTIVITIES ON THE TEACHINGS OF JESUS

LEE DANESCO

TWENTY-THIRD PUBLICATIONS
twentythirdpublications.com

Second Printing 2017

TWENTY-THIRD PUBLICATIONS
A division of Bayard
One Montauk Avenue, Suite 200
New London, CT 06320
(860) 437-3012 or (800) 321-0411
www.twentythirdpublications.com

Copyright ©2015 Lee Danesco
Permission is given to reproduce the activity pages in this book as needed for non commercial use in schools and parish religious education programs. Otherwise, no part of this publication may be reproduced in any manner without prior written permission of the publisher. Write to the Permissions Editor.

ISBN: 978-1-62785-104-6
Library of Congress Control Number: 2015939730
Printed in the U.S.A.

CONTENTS

Introduction — 5

1 DISCOVERING THE SERMON ON THE MOUNT — 6
2 WHAT MAKES US HAPPY? — 8
3 BLESSED ARE THE POOR IN SPIRIT — 10
4 BLESSED ARE THEY WHO MOURN — 12
5 BLESSED ARE THE MEEK — 14
6 BLESSED ARE THEY WHO HUNGER AND THIRST FOR RIGHTEOUSNESS — 16
7 BLESSED ARE THE MERCIFUL — 18
8 BLESSED ARE THE CLEAN OF HEART — 20
9 RECIPES FOR PEACEMAKERS — 22
10 STANDING UP FOR WHAT YOU BELIEVE — 24
11 FOLLOWING THE BEATITUDES — 26
12 THE CHALLENGE OF THE BEATITUDES — 28
13 PRACTICING THE BEATITUDES — 30
14 A BEATITUDE WALL PLAQUE — 32
15 TURNING THE OTHER CHEEK — 34
16 BECOMING THE LIGHT OF THE WORLD — 36
17 THE IMPORTANCE OF FORGIVENESS — 38
18 LOVING YOUR ENEMY — 40
19 JUDGING — 42
20 THE GOLDEN RULE — 44
21 CHOOSING FRIENDS WISELY — 46
22 THE LORD'S PRAYER REVISITED — 48
23 THE LORD'S PRAYER COLORIZED — 50
24 ARE YOU FOLLOWING JESUS OR SHOWING OFF? — 52
25 WHERE DO YOU KEEP YOUR TREASURE? — 54
26 WHOM DO YOU SERVE? — 56
27 IN GOD WE TRUST—OR DO WE? — 58
28 THE ANSWER TO OUR PRAYERS — 60
29 WHAT HOLDS YOUR LIFE TOGETHER? — 62
30 JOINING THE DISCIPLES — 64
31 THE WORK OF DISCIPLES — 66
32 HAVE YOU SEEN ANY DISCIPLES? — 68
33 MEMOS FROM THE MOUNT — 70

INTRODUCTION

Faith is the generous gift of a loving God. Nurturing the faith of children is the joy-filled responsibility of parents, catechists, the faith community, and children themselves. Providing assistance for that process is the goal of *Enriching Faith Series: Lessons, Prayers and Activities on the Teachings of Jesus*.

Drawing upon the condensed presentation of Jesus' teachings found in the Sermon on the Mount (Matthew 5—7), *Lessons, Prayers and Activities on the Teachings of Jesus* was written to fill lesson resource needs across the curriculum and throughout the catechetical year.

The first page of each two-page chapter welcomes catechists by sharing a well-defined lesson **Objective,** brief **Catechist Background,** and a detailed list of necessary **Materials.** To help catechists create student interest and motivate their participation, a **Lesson Starter** is provided. Directions for the accompanying individual or group **Activity** and a related final **Prayer** complete the outline page.

The second page of each chapter is a reproducible activity sheet that focuses on the words of Jesus where they intersect with the lives of children.

Jesus' teachings found in the Sermon on the Mount were offered for the first time to his disciples. *Lessons, Prayers and Activities on the Teachings of Jesus* attempts to forward those same words to today's disciples. That includes teachers who want the flexibility of activities that can creatively charge fifteen minutes or fill an entire class session, parents who seek reinforcement and clarification for their at-home faith sharing, and especially children who enjoy active and interactive techniques that help them transport Jesus' word off the page and into their lives.

DISCOVERING THE SERMON ON THE MOUNT

Objective
To help children locate and understand the Sermon on the Mount in Matthew 5—7, as some of Jesus' most important lessons.

Catechist background
Many of the best-known and most essential teachings of Jesus appear clustered together in Bible verses known collectively as "The Sermon on the Mount." Walking children through the process of finding the Sermon on the Mount and acquainting them with its rich content encourages them to focus attention squarely on the chapters and themes central to all remaining activities in this book.

Materials
- ☐ **Book-marked teacher's Bible**
- ☐ **Black or blue marker and crayons**
- ☐ **Lesson 1 activity worksheets**

Lesson starter
Holding up a Bible, say: *Some of the most important things that Jesus ever taught are found in the Bible in "The Sermon on the Mount." So how do we find that Sermon to learn what it's all about?* (Most young children will not know; older children may already be skilled in finding citations.)

Demonstrate how to locate the Sermon on the Mount by following these simple steps:
- Hold up a copy of the Bible.
- Indicate the small portion of the Bible that contains the New Testament.
- Show the even smaller section that holds the Gospel according to Matthew.
- Draw attention to the very few pages on which the Sermon on the Mount can be found.

Activity
Distribute Activity 1 worksheets, markers, and crayons.

Say: *The numbered squares on the worksheet represent different parts of the Bible that we pass through on our way to finding the Sermon on the Mount. Square (1) represents the complete Bible, so after (1), write "BIBLE." Continue the marking process. Square (2) represents the New Testament. Square (3) represents Matthew's gospel. And Square (4) represents the Sermon on the Mount.*

Choose four different colored crayons. Use your favorite color to shade in Square 4 (the Sermon on the Mount). Use the other crayons to shade the margins of the remaining squares.

In pairs (or small groups), *choose and discuss the meaning of any one of the teachings from the Sermon on the Mount listed on the worksheet. Be ready to share what you think the teaching means and why it seems important to you.*

Option
Students already skilled in locating Bible passages can start the lesson by finding Matthew 5—7 in their student Bible on their own and then completing the activity page.

Prayer
We thank you, Almighty Father, for your words in your holy Bible. By reading and following the teaching of Jesus, your Son, may we grow in our love for you and for our neighbor. Amen.

ACTIVITY SHEET 1

Discovering the Sermon on the Mount

CHOOSE ONE TEACHING FROM THE SERMON ON THE MOUNT →

- Blessed are the peacemakers.
- Blessed are the merciful.
- Ask and it will be given to you.
- Love your enemies.

MEANING AND IMPORTANCE

_____
_____
_____
_____

2. WHAT MAKES US HAPPY?

Objective
Present an overview that allows children to compare the ordinary paths to human happiness with the Beatitude path Jesus describes.

Catechist background
Most of us experience happiness on a regular basis. We know what makes us happy and what brings a smile to the faces of our friends.

At the beginning of the Sermon on the Mount, in verses called "the Beatitudes," Jesus asks us to look at happiness from new and unusual perspectives. He encourages us to find eternal happiness in God's kingdom by living a lifestyle built on these Beatitudes.

By keeping the Beatitudes in mind when they respond to everyday situations, children can practice the Christian way of living and investigate the unique opportunity for the happiness it promises.

Materials
- ☐ Whiteboard or flip chart and markers
- ☐ Six magazine photos of smiling people
- ☐ Lesson 2 activity worksheets
- ☐ Bible

Lesson starter
Say: *Look carefully at each picture I hold up and decide what you think might be causing each person to smile.*

On the board, write "WHAT MAKES US HAPPY." As you review the pictures, record the reasons given by the students for each individual smile.

These are good reasons for people to feel happy. At the beginning of the Sermon on the Mount, Jesus offers an entirely different list of behaviors and attitudes that he says can fill us with lasting joy. This is Jesus' list, which we call the Beatitudes. (Read aloud Matthew 5:3–12.)

Make a second list on the board titled "Beatitude Happiness," and record an abbreviated, age-appropriate version of the Beatitudes as you read them.

Are you wondering how things like being a peacemaker, showing mercy, or working hard at doing the right thing can really make us happy? The worksheet activity gives you a chance to explore the possibilities.

Activity
Say: *After reading each worksheet case, with a partner discuss and decide which of the two possible answers would best allow you to follow Jesus' teachings in the Beatitudes.*

Check student answers using the key below as needed. Discuss the reasons behind their decisions and how in each case making "Beatitude" choices would lead to happiness.

Key: 1. (b); 2. (a); 3. (b); 4. (b); 5. (b); 6. (b); 7. (a); 8. (b).

Option
Personalize the "lesson starter" by asking children, in advance, to bring in pictures in which *they* are the smiling subjects.

Prayer
Loving God, thank you for your many gifts that fill us with happiness each day. Help us to find lasting joy in your kingdom by living our lives according to the Beatitudes taught by Jesus. Amen.

What Makes Us Happy?

In each case circle either letter (A) or (B) to indicate which advice Jesus would give you to make you truly happy.

1. You had a wonderful family vacation.
- **A** No reason to thank anyone. You deserved it.
- **B** Thank your parents and thank God.

2. You take candy from the store without paying for it.
- **A** Be really sorry for what you did and pay back the owner.
- **B** Don't worry about it. It's no big deal.

3. There is a crowd of kids getting on the bus.
- **A** It's okay to push. You want a good seat.
- **B** Stay in line, don't complain, and wait your turn.

4. You forgot to study for a quiz at school.
- **A** Copy from someone else's paper. It's only a quiz.
- **B** Do your own work, even if you make mistakes.

5. At church you see a "Gloves for the Needy" basket.
- **A** Keep walking. That's someone else's problem.
- **B** Check at home for gloves you can give next week.

6. Your elderly neighbors' walk needs shoveling.
- **A** Ask them how much they can pay you to shovel it.
- **B** Shovel without pay because they need help.

7. Two of your friends are arguing angrily.
- **A** Say something positive about their friendship.
- **B** Don't butt in; it's none of your business.

8. A classmate makes fun of your religion.
- **A** Give him a shove; he's looking for trouble.
- **B** Ignore him or help him to understand your faith.

3. BLESSED ARE THE POOR IN SPIRIT
When Less Means More

Objective
Explore the meaning of the first Beatitude. Consider how pursuing fewer possessions opens up time and space to discover dependence on God, who alone offers true and lasting happiness.

Catechist background
What does Jesus mean when he teaches that being "poor" is a "blessing"? For children, his words seem a confusing contradiction. Thanks to the daily barrage of exciting new products and the advertising blitz that promotes them, children are easily convinced that buying more and more things, not less, is what will make them happy.

In the first Beatitude, Jesus challenges this attitude and asks us to consider another possibility. What if "less" can actually lead to "more"? The less our lives are cluttered with material goods and the less time we spend pursuing new possessions, the more time we free up for God and the happiness he provides.

Materials
- ☐ Lesson 3 activity worksheets
- ☐ Pencils

Lesson starter
Say: *What's better—more? or less? Most people would probably say more. Tell me what you would like more of today.*

Write responses on board.

These things are not bad in themselves, but if we spend all our time and energy trying to get and keep more and more things, we run out of time and space for God in our lives. The first Beatitude, "Blessed are the poor in spirit…," teaches us that sometimes "less" can actually give us more happiness. With fewer things, we can enjoy the true luxury of having more time for God in our lives.

Activity
Say: *In Part A on the worksheet, investigate the idea that sometimes less of one thing can surprisingly produce more of something else you truly value. Complete the first three examples and then add three examples of your own that show how sometimes less can mean more. Be ready to share your answers.*

When Part A is finished, say: *Part A has certainly showed us that less can give us more. Now let's think about how to arrange for more time in our lives for God. Under Part B, list three things that having or doing less of will allow you to have more time for God in your life.*

Option
In worksheet Part A, while working on the last three sets of blanks, ask older students to complete the "less" blanks and then exchange sheets and complete the "more" responses on the sheet they receive.

Prayer
Holy God, help us to appreciate the true value of the many good things in our lives. Then teach us to spend less time on things so we can spend more time following you. Amen.

ACTIVITY SHEET 3

Blessed Are the Poor in Spirit

WHEN LESS MEANS MORE

Part A

Less **complaining** can = more _____

Less **gossiping** can = more _____

Less **sugar** can = more _____

your examples

Less _____ can = more _____

Less _____ can = more _____

Less _____ can = more _____

Part B

Less _____ can = **more God in my life**.

Less _____ can = **more God in my life**.

Less _____ can = **more God in my life**.

BLESSED ARE THEY WHO MOURN
God Waits to Comfort the Sorrowing

Objective

Use the example of Peter's denial and Jesus' response of forgiveness and love to lend student-friendly meaning to the Beatitude "Blessed are they who mourn…"

Catechist background

Children understand "mourning." Even if their own families are safe, most young people have felt genuine sorrow for people they see in TV images of life-ending or life-altering tragedy. It's natural for children to wonder how people suffering such overwhelming losses can really be thought of as "blessed."

Peter's relationship with Jesus offers a clarifying picture. After denying Jesus three times, Peter was filled with great sadness. But after the resurrection, Jesus comforted Peter by restoring their relationship of trust and love.

Materials
- ☐ Whiteboard or flip chart and markers
- ☐ Lesson 4 activity worksheets
- ☐ Crayons or markers

Lesson starter

Say: *A simple explanation for the word "mourn" is to grieve or be very sad about a loss. Take a few minutes and ask the person next to you to describe how they think someone looks or acts when he or she is mourning.*

After this exchange, ask volunteers to share what they learned about mourning from their classmates. List these lessons on the board.

Do you think a person who fits the description on the board could be called happy? It doesn't seem that way, does it? So what is Jesus saying when he preaches: "Blessed are those who mourn, for they shall be comforted"?

The story of Jesus and his good friend Peter can help us understand why Jesus claims that the sadness of mourning could become a blessing.

Activity

Say: *The worksheet lists major changes in Peter's friendship with Jesus. Discuss each change either by reading the gospel passage or sharing your own simplified version of the same.*

Now, from the list on the left side of the page, select a word that best describes how you think Peter felt at each turning point. You can use words more than once, and some words may not be needed at all. There are no right or wrong answers. Write the words in the space provided. Use colored markers that you think best match Peter's mood or feelings at the time.

Peter's experience teaches us that we can expect sad times in our lives, but if we turn to God, we can also expect to find comfort and joy in his love.

Option

Older children can locate the Scripture passages and then complete the activity by using their own words to describe Peter's feelings at each turning point.

Prayer

Help us, Almighty Father, even when we feel sad and alone, to remember that you are always ready to welcome us and bless us with the comfort of your everlasting love. Amen.

ACTIVITY SHEET 4

Blessed Are They Who Mourn

GOD WAITS TO COMFORT THE SORROWING

Word choices

AFRAID

EXCITED

BROKEN-HEARTED

SPECIAL

BRAVE

FORGIVEN

FAITHFUL

LOVED

PROUD

PLEASED

POWERFUL

COMFORTED

LONELY

FRIGHTENED

WORRIED

Jesus calls Peter.
(MATTHEW 4:18-20)

Peter feels: _____

Peter jumps out of the boat.
(MATTHEW 14:28-30)

Peter feels: _____

Peter calls Jesus "Messiah."
(MATTHEW 16:15-16)

Peter feels: _____

Jesus calls Peter "the rock."
(MATTHEW 16:18-20)

Peter feels: _____

Peter promises to be faithful.
(MATTHEW 26:35)

Peter feels: _____

Peter denies Jesus.
(MATTHEW 26:70)

Peter feels: _____

Peter mourns over his sin.
(MATTHEW 26:75)

Peter feels: _____

Peter is welcomed back.
(JOHN 21:17)

Peter feels: _____

5 BLESSED ARE THE MEEK
The Meek Are Not Weak

Objective
Share Jesus' Beatitude message about the great joy to be found when the words and actions of our lives are flavored by meekness.

Catechist background
Children often assume that the way to get what you want is to follow the highly visible examples of aggression, arrogance, impatience, and force.

In the third Beatitude, Jesus suggests meekness as an alternative model. But when children realize that "the meek" are those marked by kindness, patience, gentleness, and respect, they may doubt the effectiveness of the meek approach to success.

By visualizing how meekness can be incorporated into the lives of both famous people and typical students, young people may rethink their attitude about the blessings of meekness.

Materials
- ☐ Lesson 5 activity worksheets
- ☐ Crayons or markers
- ☐ Clues for lesson starter
- ☐ (Optional) random props

Lesson starter
Say: *Listen to this description of a famous person, and when you think you know who I am talking about, raise your hand.*

Using simple, grade-appropriate clues, ask children to identify someone well known for his or her accomplishments but also with a reputation for meekness, kindness, or gentleness. For example, Abraham Lincoln, Martin Luther King Jr., or Mother Teresa. Once students guess correctly, list ways in which this powerful person was also someone of unusual meekness who was kind, gentle, patient, and respectful of others.

This example points out the truth that meek people who treat others with kindness, gentleness, patience, and respect can also be strong, creative, successful, and accomplished individuals.

Activity
Say: *This worksheet activity will show the positive part meekness can play in your life. On the left is a column of small sketches of places where children might spend time together. Under each setting is a word or phrase that describes meekness. Your job is to imagine what could happen in each place if, instead of being aggressive or angry, young people treated one another according to that word or phrase.*

In the available space, explain how that kind of meek action could make a better experience for the people gathered in that setting. Be ready to share your examples with the class.

Options
Older students may work as a group and act out their answers, using available props to show the value of meekness in action.

Prayer
Lord Jesus, you have blessed us with a new understanding of meekness. In the week ahead, help us to include kindness, patience, gentleness, and respect in our words and actions. Amen.

ACTIVITY SHEET 5

Blessed Are the Meek

THE MEEK ARE NOT WEAK

SETTING	POSITIVE EFFECTS OF ACTIONS
MOVIE THEATER **Respect for others**	
RESTAURANT **Patience**	
PLAYGROUND **Gentleness**	
CHURCH **Kindness**	

6 BLESSED ARE THEY WHO HUNGER AND THIRST FOR RIGHTEOUSNESS
Is Righteousness On Your Wish List?

Objective
Construct a child-friendly definition for "righteousness" by reviewing the best qualities children find in their best friends.

Catechist background
Jesus includes those who "hunger and thirst for righteousness" among those whom he calls "blessed."

Unfortunately, "righteousness" is not a word frequently used by children, but it can take on real meaning when it is viewed as a combination of the very best qualities of their best friends. Then it becomes something for which one truly hungers and thirsts.

Materials
☐ Lesson 6 activity worksheets and pencils
☐ Whiteboard or flip chart and markers

Lesson starter
Say: *Close your eyes. Imagine a situation in which you feel either very thirsty or very hungry.*

With students' eyes closed, call students by name to answer the questions below.
- *What might have caused you to be so thirsty or hungry?*
- *How long does it seem like you have gone without something to drink or eat?*
- *Right now what would you really like to drink or eat?*

Ask the students to open their eyes.

This kind of overpowering thirst and hunger is what Jesus is talking about in the Beatitudes when he says: "Blessed are they who hunger and thirst for righteousness." He hopes that you will want to have "righteousness" in your life as much as you wanted something to drink or eat just now.

So what is "righteousness"?

Activity
Say: *One way to think about righteousness is to say that it's like something you would get if you added together the best qualities of your best friends.*

On the worksheet, List A includes eight good qualities you might find in your best friends. Add two of your own ideas about what makes up a good friend in spaces 9 and 10. (Don't list "righteousness.")

Create List B by rearranging the qualities in List A according to how important these qualities are to you in choosing a friend. List the most important quality first.

Determine the top three qualities students selected. Discuss together how well these qualities define righteousness.

Options
Older students can complete this same activity while working in pairs or small groups.

Prayer
The very best qualities in our friends can help us to discover the meaning of righteousness. Help us, O Lord, to offer examples of righteousness to our friends in return. Amen.

ACTIVITY SHEET 6

Blessed Are They Who Hunger and Thirst for Righteousness

IS RIGHTEOUSNESS ON YOUR WISH LIST?

LIST A

Polite
Kind
Fair
Smart
Generous
Loyal
Honest
Caring
_____
_____

LIST B

7 BLESSED ARE THE MERCIFUL
Smoothing the Path for Others

Objective
Provide students with an opportunity to recognize the needs of others around them and to consider merciful responses that might help to meet those needs.

Catechist background
Too often when we see someone enduring hardships, we feel an immediate wave of pity but then return our focus to whatever we're doing at the time. In the fifth Beatitude, "Blessed are the merciful," Jesus is asking us to do much more.

Being merciful requires a two-part response—feeling compassion *and* taking action. By giving compassionate consideration to the bumps along life's journey, children sharpen their awareness of the real difficulties people face every day. Planning how to reduce the suffering and hardships of others allows children to see that being merciful calls upon us to act.

Materials
- ☐ Lesson 7 activity worksheets
- ☐ Whiteboard or flip chart and markers
- ☐ Markers for children

Lesson starter
Say: *When was the last time you took a walk or hike with your family or friends? Where did you go? What made it fun?* (Encourage volunteer responses.)

As enjoyable as hikes and walks can be, we sometimes run into difficulties. Take a minute and look out the window; imagine yourself on the last walk you took. Call to mind any problems, large or small, that you or your companions faced along the way.

While children are thinking, draw a line on the board similar to the path on the worksheet. Call on student volunteers to share a problem they remember from their walk. Summarize their comments in a few words and write them along the path you have drawn.

Activity
Say: *The path drawn on your worksheet is not a hiking trail. It's a trail that represents the life path of any family. Notice the "bump" marks on the line. They are reminders that life is not always smooth or easy. In pairs or small groups, imagine the kinds of real-life difficulties typical families often face. Write a short description of each problem on one of the lines on one side of the path.*

Let's share and compare what you have noted.

Now go back to the worksheet and next to each "difficulty," suggest ways in which other individuals, families, or the parish community might offer to help people over that particular bump.

Option
Direct small groups to write down difficulties families face on one side of the path. To gather suggestions for merciful responses to those problems, ask students to pass their worksheets to one or more other groups. Share the results.

Prayer
Teach us, Merciful Father, to remember the many needs of others at home, at school, and in the world around us. Help us, Lord, to act mercifully to reduce the suffering and hardship felt by those in need. Amen.

ACTIVITY SHEET 7

Blessed Are the Merciful
SMOOTHING THE PATH FOR OTHERS

DIFFICULTY:
_____
_____
_____

DIFFICULTY:
_____
_____
_____

DIFFICULTLY:
_____
_____
_____

DIFFICULTY:
_____
_____
_____

8. BLESSED ARE THE CLEAN OF HEART

Objective
Rely on the easy comparison of "house cleaning" and "heart cleaning" to guide children through the sixth Beatitude—"Blessed are the clean of heart."

Catechist background
Children are well-schooled in the meaning of the word "clean." They hear it regularly, usually followed by words like "your room," "your clothes," or "the garage."

Jesus attaches new meaning to the word "clean" by connecting it directly to the condition of our hearts. When he announces, "Blessed are the clean of heart," the cleanliness he has in mind has little to do with physical or material things but a good deal to do with our inner relationship with God.

Reviewing the everyday steps involved in cleaning their homes can help open children's eyes to steps they might also take to tidy up their relationship with God.

Materials
- ☐ Lesson 8 activity worksheets
- ☐ Markers
- ☐ Stickers

Lesson starter
Write on the board: "I want you to go and clean your_____."

Say: *When you hear your parents say those words to you, how do they often fill in the blank?* (Encourage volunteer answers.) *Probably your parents have good reasons for their suggestions, but Jesus would fill in the blank with a different and probably unexpected word.*

In the Beatitudes, Jesus tells us, "Blessed are the clean in heart." Jesus is calling on us to go beyond our regular household cleaning chores to take care of the obstacles, distractions, and sinfulness that may be cluttering up our relationship with God—or what Jesus simply calls our "heart."

Activity
Say: *You can go about the task of cleaning up your hearts in much the same way you go about cleaning at home.*

Under the title "Cleaning," your worksheet is divided between "house" cleaning and "heart" cleaning. This chart can help you recognize the similarities and differences between cleaning a room in your home and tidying up your friendship with God.

First answer questions about how you go about cleaning a room, and then answer the same questions as they connect to cleaning up your heart.

When all have finished, discuss together the similarities and differences that appear between the two distinct types of cleaning activities.

Option
Ask younger students to place a sticker either at the bottom of the left or right column to indicate whether they believe they usually do better cleaning their "house" or their "heart." Together, consider ways to improve our approaches to cleaning the heart.

Prayer
Loving God, help us to direct our attention each day toward removing those things in our lives that can keep us from fully loving and serving you. Amen.

ACTIVITY SHEET 8

Blessed Are the Clean of Heart

	🏠	♥
When?		
Who?		
How? (tools)		
Difficulty		
Results/rewards		

9 RECIPES FOR PEACEMAKERS

Objective
Examine the ingredients that go into the everyday work of being the kind of "peacemaker" Jesus blesses in the Beatitudes.

Catechist background
Children recognize the difference between a pleasant conversation and one filled with anger. Most children also know what a "recipe" is and how important it can be, even in the preparation of something as basic as a sandwich.

When used in tandem, these two seemingly unrelated bits of knowledge give children effective means to understand and live the seventh Beatitude.

Materials
- ☐ Focus pictures and pencils
- ☐ Lesson 9 activity worksheets

Lesson Starter
Give pairs of students newspaper or magazine pictures of people either obviously enjoying each other's company or in full-blown disagreement with one another.

Say: *Jesus says, "Blessed are the peacemakers." Look at the picture you have been given. Do you think the people in your picture are peacemakers or people who need a peacemaker? Explain the reasons for your answer.* (Take volunteer responses.)

At school, with friends, or at home, we can often tell when we need a "peacemaker," but it's more difficult to know how to actually go about being the peacemaker and helping to make the peace. Well, maybe not as difficult as you think.

You all know how to make a sandwich. As long as you follow the simple recipe and use the right ingredients, you can produce a tasty sandwich. But what happens to the taste of your favorite sandwich if you change the recipe and add some of the wrong ingredients? (Ask for some examples.)

Activity
Say: *Using the right ingredients is just as important for making and keeping the peace in conversations as it is for making a good sandwich. Look at RECIPE #1 on your worksheet. Read through the list of ingredients that you are told to add to a normal conversation. Then, at the end of the list, after the word "Results," write how you think this conversation will end.*

In RECIPE #2, add a different set of ingredients that you believe will help move the conversation along to a better end.

Share and compare your recipes for peace.

Option
Ask older students to use their recipe once at home or among friends and report the results at the next meeting.

Prayer
God of peace and harmony, help us when we feel angry, or see others who are angry, to have the patience and courage to put unkind words and actions aside and use a recipe for peace. Amen.

ACTIVITY SHEET 9

Recipes for Peacemakers

Recipe #1

DIRECTIONS: add the following ingredients to a normal conversation and mix

INGREDIENTS
1. Make mean or frightening faces
2. Lean forward into the other person's space
3. Talk in a very loud, deep, or high-pitched voice
4. Raise a hand or clenched fist
5. Use mean, unkind, or hurtful words

RESULTS
_____
_____
_____
_____
_____

Recipe #2

DIRECTIONS: add the following ingredients to a normal conversation and mix

INGREDIENTS
1. _____
2. _____
3. _____
4. _____
5. _____

RESULTS
_____
_____
_____
_____
_____

10 STANDING UP FOR WHAT YOU BELIEVE

Objective
Break open the issue of "persecution": how it can affect children, and how they can respond if and when it occurs.

Catechist background
People who feel challenged by the beliefs of others sometimes strike back with acts of persecution, such as unkind words, threats, or even violence.

In the final two Beatitudes, Jesus calls upon his followers to expect, accept, and work through the persecution that may come their way when they share his message or mention his name. Learning how to respond when they are insulted, made fun of, or pressured to ignore Jesus and his teachings are valuable lessons for children who wish to be faithful followers of Jesus.

Materials
- ☐ Whiteboard or flip chart and markers
- ☐ Lesson 10 activity worksheets
- ☐ Crayons or markers
- ☐ Bible

Lesson starter
Say: *Raise your hand if you have ever seen someone on TV or in a movie who has been picked on, made fun of, or threatened because of what he or she believes.* (Ask volunteers to share examples.) *The stories you shared remind us of what persecution looks like and how it can make someone feel. Jesus talks to us about persecution in the last two Beatitudes.* (Read Mt 5: 10–11.)

As followers of Jesus, we are expected to share his teachings openly in all we say and do. But Jesus tells us not everyone will like our words or actions. Those who don't understand our faith or feel challenged by it might make fun of us or try to turn us away from our faith.

We can stand up for our faith by using words and actions that demonstrate clearly what we believe in and who we really are.

Activity
Say: *People who feel strongly about something will sometimes write their feelings in a few well-chosen words on a poster. For example, they might direct people's attention to littering issues with words like "Save the Bay." Can you think of some examples you have seen?*

If you wanted to remind other young Christians how to speak or act towards those who might be persecuting them, what kind of poster would you write?

Together as a class create six to eight such poster slogans and list them on the board.

Select your four favorite slogans from those on the board or replace with some of your own ideas. Use markers or crayons to write one slogan on each small poster board on the worksheet. Share your completed work with the class.

Option
Work in pairs or small groups to reproduce the poster and add design details on a full-sized poster board.

Prayer
Loving Father, keep us strong in our faith. Give us the courage to stand up for Jesus and his teachings in ways that show our love of God and neighbor. Amen.

ACTIVITY SHEET 10

Standing Up for What You Believe

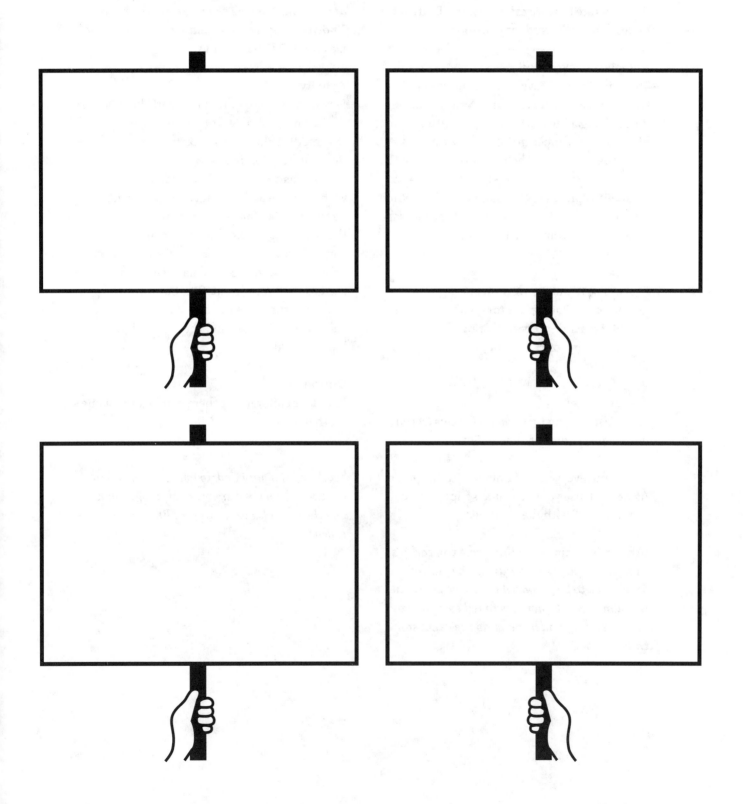

11. FOLLOWING THE BEATITUDES

Objective
Use the children's game of "Simon Says" to demonstrate how we can follow the Beatitudes of Jesus in both words and actions.

Catechist background
The game "Simon Says" invites children to hear what the leader says and copy what the leader does. Living a life based on the Beatitudes can hinge on the same principle.

Gospel images can help children observe that what Jesus preaches in the Beatitudes is also what Jesus practices throughout his life. When we both hear and see Jesus' Beatitude message in action, it becomes easier to follow his call.

Materials
- ☐ Lesson 11 activity worksheets
- ☐ Sufficient floor space for game
- ☐ Brief teacher-prepared script for basic game of "Simon Says"
- ☐ Markers

Lesson starter
Say: *We are going to warm up for this lesson with a quick game of "Simon Says."*

Make sure everyone is familiar with the game. As needed, use your prepared script to play "Simon Says" with the children.

(After a few games): *In this game you can see that the person who is playing the part of Simon has to be prepared to do two things at the same time. Simon has to tell everyone to do something, and he must do the exact same thing himself.*

Jesus teaches us to live the Beatitudes in the same way. He tells us by his preaching, and at the same time he shows us by how he lives. Knowing this, we can create a learning game we might call "Jesus Says."

Activity
Down the left column of the worksheet is a list of the Beatitudes. Next to each Beatitude, in the middle column, is an example of how Jesus lived out the Beatitude.

Work as a class to fill in the final column with a simple action that could represent each Beatitude (like folding your hands). Practice the action signs together and then try out the game. Say: *Jesus says: "Be merciful."* Everyone should follow you as you make the sign you created to represent "merciful." Continue the game following the same rules as "Simon Says" but substituting "Jesus" and the action signs you have created.

Option
For older children, let them conduct the game on their own.

Prayer
Teach us, Almighty God, to follow Jesus' call to Beatitude living, not simply because of what he preached but also because of the life he lived. Amen.

ACTIVITY SHEET 11

Following the Beatitudes

WHAT JESUS SAID "BLESSED ARE....	WHAT JESUS DID	SIGN
Those who mourn	Wept over Jerusalem **(LUKE 19:41)**	
The merciful	Forgave those who crucified him **(LUKE 23:34)**	
The clean of heart	Didn't give in to temptations **(MATTHEW 4:1)**	
The peacemakers	Forbade violence by Apostles **(MATTHEW 26:52)**	
The meek	Quietly suffered bad treatment by soldiers **(MARK 15:16–20)**	
The poor in spirit	The boy Jesus in the temple **(LUKE 2:48–49)**	
The persecuted	Jesus arrested **(LUKE 22:48–52)**	
Those who hunger and thirst for righteousness	Jesus fasting **(LUKE 4:1–2)**	

12. THE CHALLENGE OF THE BEATITUDES

Objective
Widen knowledge of the Beatitudes with an exercise that presents the challenges in each Beatitude.

Catechist background
Being able to name and explain the Beatitudes is a wonderful way to start connecting with the core teachings of Jesus. The Beatitudes take on fuller, more personal meaning when they are transferred from the page to real life.

Using a comparative exercise, students review their knowledge of the Beatitudes, compare the demands that each Beatitude places upon behavior, and gain a fuller awareness of the implications of Beatitude living.

Materials
- ☐ Lesson 12 activity worksheets
- ☐ Whiteboard or flip chart and markers
- ☐ Scissors
- ☐ Flat working surface

Lesson starter
Say: *Working together, let's see how many of the Beatitudes we can list on the board.* (Write correct answers on board.) *Some Beatitudes are difficult to understand, and some are difficult to follow in our daily lives. Today's activity is going to let us look at both kinds of Beatitudes.*

Activity
Students should work in pairs or small groups.

Say: *Cut the worksheet from one side to the other to form eight individual strips, with each strip showing one simplified Beatitude.*

On a flat surface, place strips, in no particular order, in a vertical line, so that all Beatitudes can be easily read. Move strips around and place according to how difficult they are to understand, with most difficult at the top and easiest at the bottom.

When all have completed their lineup, take time to create together a brief explanation of the meaning of each Beatitude and write the meanings on the appropriate strip.

Now rearrange the strips again according to how difficult or easy they are for children to follow in day-to-day living. This time put the easiest at the top and the most difficult at the bottom. Be ready to share your reasons with the class.

Option
Younger students can complete the same activity working alone. Their efforts should be aided by ongoing class discussion and teacher direction. When finished, students can compare their lines with those of neighboring students.

Prayer
Heavenly Father, give us the strength and courage to follow your Son, Jesus, and to live each day according to the Beatitude message he shared. Amen.

ACTIVITY SHEET 12

The Challenge of the Beatitudes

Blessed are the poor in spirit

Blessed are they who mourn

Blessed are the meek

Blessed are they who hunger and thirst for righteousness

Blessed are the merciful

Blessed are the clean of heart

Blessed are the peacemakers

Blessed are they who are persecuted for the sake of righteousness or because of me

13 PRACTICING THE BEATITUDES

Objective
Focus student attention on incorporating the Beatitudes into their daily lives through practice.

Catechist background
The Beatitudes are a collection of Jesus' teachings that highlight behaviors, attitudes, and approaches that make up a Christian way of life. If children are to follow Jesus' call to live the Beatitudes, practice is surely necessary. By creating their own Beatitude practice schedule, children make living them a regular way of life.

Materials
- ☐ Lesson 13 activity worksheets
- ☐ Whiteboard or flip charts and markers

Lesson starter
Say: *If I wanted to learn how to play baseball, what skills would I need to develop?* (Write volunteer responses on board.) *How would I go about improving my skills? ... That's right: practice. But how often do you need to practice these skills?* (Write suggestions on board and conclude that *regular practice* works better than occasional practice.) *The same thing is true when it comes to learning how to live the Beatitudes. The only way you can move forward from simply knowing the Beatitudes to being really good at living them is also through practice, regular practice. Creating your own Beatitude Practice Sheet can be a sensible way to organize your efforts.*

Activity
With the help of the sample answers below, work with children to write brief explanations for each Beatitude in the space provided on their worksheets.

POOR IN SPIRIT—*recognize the need for God in your life*

MOURNING—*show compassion for those who are suffering loss*

MEEK—*act in ways that are humble and not aggressive*

HUNGER AND THIRST FOR RIGHTEOUSNESS—*seek justice*

MERCIFUL—*care for the needs of others*

CLEAN OF HEART—*keep your heart set on God*

PEACEMAKER—*help to end arguments or tension*

PERSECUTED—*do what you know is right even if it is unpopular*

Say: *You can begin practicing the Beatitudes during the week ahead* (or any time period that best benefits your students and enhances your teaching schedule). *From the list, select any four Beatitudes you would like to work on. Then fill in the activity chart that follows. Be ready to discuss your results when we meet next.*

Option
Ask younger children to complete this activity by working on only one or two Beatitudes.

Prayer
Please help us, Jesus, to be faithful to the regular practice of the Beatitudes, knowing that it is in living your teachings that we may come to better love and serve you and our neighbor. Amen.

ACTIVITY SHEET 13

Practicing the Beatitudes

Blessed are those who (are)

Poor in spirit: _____

Mourn: _____

Meek: _____

**Hunger and thirst
for righteousness:** _____

Merciful: _____

Clean of Heart: _____

Peacemakers: _____

Persecuted: _____

DURING PRACTICE WEEK I WILL TRY TO:

1

_____
_____
_____
_____

2

_____
_____
_____
_____

3

_____
_____
_____
_____

4

_____
_____
_____
_____

14 A BEATITUDE WALL PLAQUE

Objective
Create a wall plaque to enhance the class prayer area and serve as a reminder of Jesus' call to Beatitude living.

Catechist background
The full power of the Beatitudes is most visible when they are seen together, as an interconnected and united display of the meaning of Christian living.

Engage the children in a cooperative effort to create a Beatitude wall plaque. Once assembled, the plaque can be placed in the class prayer corner as a reminder of the kind of life to which we are called as followers of Jesus.

Materials
- ☐ Whiteboard or flip chart and markers
- ☐ Lesson 14 activity worksheets
- ☐ Beatitude assignment cards
- ☐ Markers, scissors, colored paper, glitter pens, and other decorative items
- ☐ Tape or stapler

Lesson starter
Say: *I need a volunteer who is very good at walking.* (Select one volunteer.) *Please walk around the classroom just once: first at normal pace, now a little faster, now a lot slower.*

Everyone saw our walker walking. What part of him/her actually did the walking? (Take volunteer answers.) *The truth is **all** of him/her did the walking. Sure, the feet moved, but so did the legs, knees, hips, and arms: the whole body is involved. If a part of the body is not strong and healthy, the ability of the whole body to walk is affected.*

*Jesus preached **all** of the Beatitudes because they all work together to help us live as his followers.*

Activity
Say: *We can show how closely connected the Beatitudes are and how they work together by creating a wall plaque for our prayer corner.*

Distribute to each pair of students a previously prepared card with a Beatitude written on it.

On your card is one of the Beatitudes. Your job is to use your worksheet to create a square for our plaque that represents just that Beatitude.

Offer suggestions for completing the square using the art materials. Students might use block letters against a shaded background, a related symbol, or perhaps letters against a rainbow or any other natural backdrop. Squares can be as simple or as elaborate as desired. When all squares are completed, collect and tape or staple them together to form a plaque. Place the plaque in the prayer corner.

Option
For older students, worksheets can serve as models for larger poster board squares and a much larger plaque.

Prayer
Heavenly Father, working together, we have created a reminder of the Beatitudes shared by your Son, Jesus Christ. Help us to recall, live, and share these teachings each day. Amen.

ACTIVITY SHEET 14

A Beatitude Wall Plaque

15 TURNING THE OTHER CHEEK

Objective
Teach what it means to turn the other cheek through a comparative word game.

Catechist background
The phrase "an eye for an eye and a tooth for a tooth" was part of an ancient code of law. While it was seen as a justifiable way to settle a score, it also encouraged vengeance and even violence. Jesus suggests a very different response to the suffering caused by an injustice. By "turning the other cheek," we practice forgiveness and mercy, thus putting an end to settling scores.

Materials
- ☐ Lesson 15 activity worksheets
- ☐ Pencils or markers
- ☐ Whiteboard or flip chart and markers
- ☐ The following messages written on two slips of paper: "untie his/her shoe" and "pull cap over his/her eyes"
- ☐ Bible with Matthew 5:38–39 marked
- ☐ Two baseball caps

Lesson starter
Say: *I need two volunteers. Please be seated next to each other. I'm going to ask you to help us see what "evening the score" looks like. Volunteer #1: please read this slip of paper to yourself and then do what it says to Volunteer #2.* (Slip: Untie his/her shoe) *Okay, #2, please even the score.*

Repeat the process by giving the baseball caps to both children and the second slip of paper to volunteer #2 and asking volunteer #1 to even the score.

Thank you for demonstrating what it means to "even the score." Getting back at someone else can just be silly, like what we saw here. But sometimes getting even can lead us to do hurtful things. In the Sermon on the Mount, Jesus warns Christians not to seek revenge as a way to pay others back for what they have done to us.

Read aloud Matthew 5:38–39. *Today's activity lets us compare the different results that come from trying to get revenge and trying to forgive.*

Activity
Distribute the worksheets. Divide the class into two groups and invite them to gather on opposite sides of the room.

Say: *Everyone fold your worksheets along the dotted line. Group 1, your job is to look only at the "revenge" side of the paper. Use each of the letters that spell revenge (down the side of the page) to begin words or phrases that show the hurtful results that come from seeking revenge.*

Group 2, look only at the "forgive" side. Use each of the letters that spell out "forgive" to begin words or phrases that show the loving results that come when we forgive.

Give a board example of this exercise. When both groups have finished, share results.

Option
Older students might leave the page unfolded and compete to complete both sides within a set time limit.

Prayer
Forgiving Father, give us the courage and patience to move away from revenge and toward forgiveness, because by loving others, we show our love for you. Amen

ACTIVITY SHEET 15

Turn the Other Cheek

Hurtful results from revenge

R
E
V
E
N
G
E

Loving results from forgiveness

F
O
R
G
I
V
E

16 BECOMING THE LIGHT OF THE WORLD

Objective
Lead children to explore what it means to be "the light of the world" and how they can answer Jesus' call to let their own "light" shine.

Catechist background
Jesus explains that his disciples must go far beyond simply believing the words he preaches. The calling of every true follower, then and now, is to share Jesus' teachings by letting their own good deeds shine forth in places where they can be seen and experienced by others.

As they complete the worksheet, children will discover the places where the light provided by their good works can fulfill this Christian mission.

Materials
- ☐ Lesson 16 activity worksheets
- ☐ Markers or crayons
- ☐ Whiteboard or flip chart and markers
- ☐ Bible marked at Matthew 5:14–16

Lesson starter
Say: *Please close your eyes and imagine walking around inside and outside of your house. Concentrate on finding the lights in each area.*

Open your eyes and help make a list on the board of the kinds of lights you found. We can extend this list by including light sources you use when the power goes out.

In the Sermon on the Mount, Jesus adds to our list of lights. (Read Mt 5:14–16.)

In this reading, Jesus says that "You" are the light of the world. He encourages us all to do more than just understand and believe in his teachings. Through our good words and deeds, we can bring Jesus' message into our daily lives and truly light up the world for others.

Activity
Say: *From the list of light sources on the board, select one to serve as a symbol of you and the light you can shine. Draw that symbol on the worksheet under the words "Let My Light" and direct the light downward toward the words "Shine Here."*

Below the words "Shine Here," draw or write about a place where you spend time with family, friends, or even people you don't know very well.

Under the words "Through These Good Actions of Mine," list the good things you can do or say to shine light on the place and people you have sketched above. Be ready to share your work.

Option
Older children complete this activity and use it as the basis for a prayer of petition in which each student asks for the wisdom to shine his or her light on the particular situation, using the actions they noted on the worksheet.

Prayer
Almighty Father, your Son, Jesus, has told us that we are the light of the world. Help us to use good words and works to shine a light that will lead others to know and love you. Amen.

ACTIVITY SHEET 16

Becoming the Light of the World

Let my light...

shine here...

through these good actions of mine.

17 THE IMPORTANCE OF FORGIVENESS

Objective
Consider the importance of Jesus' call for reconciliation and the tools that can help us to accomplish that goal.

Catechist background
Most children have been taught that saying or doing mean things to others is not acceptable and that a sincere apology for unkind behaviors is in order. What children might not understand is how important that apology is, not just to the other person, but also to God.

In the Sermon on the Mount, Jesus explains that God is more pleased when we go and search out forgiveness from those we have hurt than he is by any gifts that we might bring to his altar. Still, understanding God's priorities—reconciliation before gifts—doesn't necessarily make it any easier for us to ask for forgiveness.

Children can take a positive approach to reconciling with others by considering, on paper, the items they would find most necessary to "pack up" for a trip to find forgiveness.

Materials
- ☐ **Lesson 17 activity worksheets**
- ☐ **Crayons, markers**
- ☐ **Whiteboard or flip chart and markers**
- ☐ **Bible**

Lesson starter
Write horizontally across the board: "T-shirt," "computer game," "movie tickets," "gift card" (or other age-appropriate gift items).

Say: *Pretend that your birthday is coming soon and people want to know what to get for you. Of the gifts listed on the board, which would be your first choice?*

Take a hand count of class responses.

There are no bad choices on this list. The choice you made tells us what your priority is, what is most important to you.

God, the Father, has priorities too. Listen to this gospel passage and see if you can figure out what God wants from us more than anything else.

Read Matthew 5:23–24. Lead the children to recognize that more than any other gift, God wants us to seek forgiveness from those we treat unkindly.

Activity
Say: *On your activity sheet look at the tools people might use to ask someone for forgiveness. Select five tools that you would unpack and use first to resolve differences.*

Write the words you choose on the five lines on the bottom half of the worksheet. After each word, tell how each particular word might help you to gain forgiveness and rebuild a relationship.

Option
Older students may read through the word choices but also include and explain others of their own.

Prayer
Merciful God, sometimes it's very hard to ask for forgiveness. Please help me to choose those tools that will remove differences with others to rebuild friendship and peace. Amen.

ACTIVITY SHEET 17

The Importance of Forgiveness

PATIENCE • CARING • HONESTY • GENTLENESS
LISTENING • DETERMINATION • KINDNESS • WISDOM
PRAYER • ENERGY • LOVE • COOPERATION • FAITH
GENEROSITY • UNDERSTANDING • SORROW FOR ACTIONS

1. _____

2. _____

3. _____

4. _____

5. _____

18 LOVING YOUR ENEMY
When Being Christian Isn't Easy

Objective
Use dialogs to demonstrate how to face and resolve the challenges we meet while attempting to follow Jesus' call to love our enemies.

Catechist background
Dialogs using stuffed animals or other toy figures offer a gentle, even amusing, medium through which children can explore Jesus' difficult teaching about loving those who may be mean or unkind to us or to those we love.

In everyday settings, children can consider what unkindness looks and feels like and the different outcomes that can result when we respond to unkindness with love not hate.

Materials
- ☐ Bible
- ☐ **Stuffed animals, dolls, or hand puppets, one per child**
- ☐ Lesson 18 activity worksheets

Lesson starter
Say: *How do you make your friends happy?* (Take volunteer answers.) *We all have examples of how we are kind to our friends. Listen to how Jesus asks us to do something more.* (Read aloud Matthew 5:44–45.) *If we want to follow Jesus, we need to think about how we can love even those who are unkind to us.*

Activity
Divide students into small groups or pairs and equip each child with a worksheet and a stuffed animal, doll, or hand puppet.

Say: *Imagine your stuffed animals taking part in each of the "Unpleasant Encounters with the Unkind" settings on the worksheet. In each encounter, one stuffed animal is being treated unkindly by the other. Neither of the stuffed animals has ever heard about Jesus or about "loving your enemy."*

Use your stuffed animals to create a conversation based on the unkind words or actions. Show how the animal being treated unkindly might react. Remember: No one in this conversation knows anything about Jesus' command to love your enemies.

Invite the children to share their dialogs with the class.

What happened when one of the stuffed animals responded to someone else's unkindness with their own unkind words or actions?

(After the children have shared about this:) Now repeat the same scenes, but pretend that the animal that is being treated unkindly knows and believes in Jesus' call to love our enemies. So have the animal respond to unkindness by using one or more of the Christian responses listed on the worksheet or by adding your own Christian responses to the conversation.

Share second set of dialogs.

What difference did responding with Christian love make in what started out to be an unpleasant encounter?

Option
Older children may choose to present original conversations based on scenarios of "unpleasant encounters" that are age appropriate and catechist approved.

Prayer
Loving God, give me patience and courage to follow the call of your Son, Jesus, to answer evil with good, and meanness with kindness, and so turn hate into love. Amen.

ACTIVITY SHEET 18

Loving Your Enemy
WHEN BEING CHRISTIAN ISN'T EASY

Unpleasant encounters with the unkind

- Someone pushes in front of you in lunch line
- Someone says something unkind about your family
- Someone makes fun of your religion
- Someone calls you a very mean name for no reason.

Christian responses to those who act unkindly

- Try to understand or sympathize with them
- Speak to them in a kind and gentle voice
- Be patient with them
- Offer them help with whatever is bothering them
- Pray for them and forgive them

Your ideas: _____

19 JUDGING
Whose Job Is It?

Objective
Learn to divide the job of judging according to *what* is being judged.

Catechist background
When Jesus tells his followers to "Stop judging," he calls attention to the fact that there are two kinds of judgments. Some judging, like that applied by legal authorities, can be accomplished fairly through diligent use of human intelligence and existing technology. Other judging requires information only available to God. In those cases God alone can judge correctly.

Learning and observing the boundaries between these two kinds of judgments comes with practice and prayer.

Materials
- ☐ Whiteboard or flip chart and markers
- ☐ Marked copy of Bible
- ☐ Lesson 19 activity worksheets
- ☐ Stickers—one set representing "God"; one set representing people

Lesson starter
Say: *Take three minutes to talk to your neighbor about the things kids might do in your school that could get them in trouble. Now help me list them on the board.*

Fortunately, we have teachers, principals and superintendents who judge what should happen to children when they misbehave in school. They make these judgments in order to keep you safe.

In the Sermon on the Mount (Matthew 7:1), *Jesus says "Stop judging." What do you think Jesus means by this? What kind of "judging" do you think he is talking about?*

Lead discussion to reveal two kinds of judging: judgments that people make, and those judgments that require knowledge possessed only by God. Point out that only God can judge what is in our hearts.

Activity
Say: *Read each situation on your worksheet and decide who should do the judging. On the line before each situation write either "G," if God should judge, or "P," if people are able to judge. Be ready to share reasons for your choices.*

When finished, ask students to review and correct worksheets with your direction.

I am passing out two sets of stickers; one represents God, and the other represents people. (Indicate which is which.) *Place a sticker after each situation to correctly show who should be the judge.*

Option
Older students complete the top half of the worksheet and then create their own examples for the bottom half.

Prayer
Almighty Father, help us to remember that only you know what is in the hearts and minds of all your children. Then keep us from making judgments that belong to you alone. Amen.

ACTIVITY SHEET 19

Judging

WHOSE JOB IS IT?

Mark each of the following with either a "G" for God or a "P" for people to identify who should be the judge.

____ The best-tasting blueberry pie

____ The fastest runner

____ How sorry someone is

____ Who loves God

____ If someone is generous

____ If someone has a fever

____ If a driver is speeding

____ Why someone lost their temper

Create three different situations that can correctly be judged by →

PEOPLE

1. _____
2. _____
3. _____

GOD

1. _____
2. _____
3. _____

THE GOLDEN RULE
How Do You Want to Be Treated?

Objective
Explain the way we should treat others by first reexamining the way we truly wish to be treated ourselves.

Catechist background
The "Golden Rule" is a widely known and frequently used moral command about treating others the way we want to be treated. It is used by Jesus in the Sermon on the Mount (Matthew 7:12).

Just like other frequently used phrases, the Golden Rule can become so commonplace that it begins to lose its vitality and effectiveness. Given the chance to reflect on how they honestly do wish to be treated by other people, children can learn to respond more successfully to the serious behavioral challenge that the Golden Rule presents.

Materials
☐ **Magnifying glass or binoculars**
☐ **Objects to magnify and examine**
☐ **Lesson 20 activity worksheets**

Lesson starter
Hold up (or indicate outside) an object for children to examine.

Say: *Using your normal eyesight describe the object you see: its size, shape, color, or other features.* (Record on the board.) *Look at the same object again only this time through a magnifying lens or binoculars. What can you add to the description on the board?* (Draw a line under the first things written and record additions.)

How has the lens/binoculars changed your idea or impression of the object? That's right; the object remains the same, but now we can see and understand it better.

The Golden Rule helps us to use a kind of magnifying glass when we look at the world around us. In the Sermon on the Mount, Jesus tells us: "Do to others what you would have them do to you." Until we have really magnified an action and looked closely at how it would make us feel, we shouldn't take that action toward anyone else.

Activity
Distribute worksheets and ask students to immediately fold the sheet in half along the fold line so that the top of the printed side is showing.

Looking only at the top half of the worksheet, read each situation and write how you hope other people will treat you in each case. (Review responses.)

Now flip the paper over to show just the bottom half of the printed page. Write how you now think you should treat other people for the things that they might do. (Review responses.)

Giving serious thought to how we want to be treated can help us to see more clearly how Christ calls us to treat others.

Option
Older students may create and act out their own scenarios to demonstrate the differences that sometimes exist between how we wish to be treated and how we actually do treat others.

Prayer
Clear our sight, Almighty Father, so that by looking first at the treatment we want for ourselves, we can more clearly see the treatment we should give to our neighbors. Amen.

ACTIVITY SHEET 20

The Golden Rule

HOW DO YOU WANT TO BE TREATED?

How do you really want people to treat you if:

You forget to call them after school?

You aren't feeling well and ignore them?

You spill your lunch—all over them?

You get very angry over nothing and take it out on them?

What should you do to others if:

They forget to call you after school?

They aren't feeling well and ignore you?

They spill their lunch in the cafeteria—on you?

They get very angry over nothing and take it out on you?

CHOOSING FRIENDS WISELY

Objective
Present Jesus' words in the Sermon on the Mount as a helpful guide for selecting good friends.

Catechist background
Children don't grow up in isolation. What they learn and how they apply it is greatly influenced by the many hours they spend with friends and by the kind of friends they select. Because the process of choosing good friends can be influenced by arrangements as random as a shared homeroom or carpool, guidelines can be helpful.

For young people, learning how to sort through many potential companions and single out those most likely to be kind, compassionate, and gospel-centered can begin by recalling a simple observation that Jesus shares in the Sermon on the Mount: "By their fruits you will know them" (Matthew 7:20).

Materials
☐ Whiteboard or flip chart and markers
☐ Markers
☐ Lesson 21 activity worksheets

Lesson starter
Say: *How many hours do you spend with your friends each day?* (Write the average answer on the board.) *Let's multiply that by seven days in a week* (on the board). *The answer is the amount of time you spend with friends during one week. Multiply that by fifty-two and we see about how much time you spend with friends in a year* (on the board). *So you can see how important it is to choose your friends carefully.*

Jesus worried about the kinds of people his followers might meet. He wanted to help them avoid those who would try to lead them away from God.

Activity
Say: *Jesus explained how to recognize, and so avoid, people who could cause you harm when he said: "By their fruits you will know them." It was his way of saying that what people say and do tells us a lot about who they really are.*

At the top of the worksheet, listed under "Student Behavior," are ten ways boys and girls act that tell us a lot about them. Read each behavior and then take the number of the behavior and write it inside an apple on either the "Good Tree" or the "Bad Tree." Make sure that all the fruit that is good is on the Good Tree and that the fruit that is bad is on the Bad Tree. Which tree (person) would you pick for a friend?

Option
Create a list of ten additional behaviors and use to enlarge activity as above.

Prayer
Teach us, Loving God, to choose friends whose words and actions give constant proof of their goodness. Amen.

ACTIVITY SHEET 21

Choosing Friends Wisely

STUDENT BEHAVIOR

1. often in trouble
2. obeys parents
3. uses bad words
4. bullies younger kids
5. volunteers to help
6. follows the rules
7. goes to church
8. never shares
9. tries hard
10. chooses mean friends

**Good Fruit
= Good Tree**

**Bad Fruit
= Bad Tree**

THE LORD'S PRAYER REVISITED

Objective
To refresh and renew student understanding of the words of the Lord's Prayer.

Catechist background
We are all familiar with the Lord's Prayer, the words Jesus gave as a model to assist us in prayer. It can be challenging to hold on to the meaning, sincerity, and intensity of a prayer so frequently offered.

By occasionally revisiting powerful phrases of the Lord's Prayer through a question and answer activity, children can develop a deeper understanding of, and enthusiasm for, the prayer we hold sacred.

Materials
☐ Whiteboard or flip chart and markers
☐ Lesson 22 activity worksheets

Lesson starter
Write on board: "allegiance" "republic" "indivisible."

Say: *Who can tell me where we can find these words used together. That's right—in the Pledge of Allegiance. Who on the left side of the room can tell me what "allegiance" means? Who on the right side of the room can explain the word "republic"? Who on either side can tell us about the word "indivisible"?*

We hear and say the Pledge of Allegiance so often it's easy for us to lose track of those key words sometimes and just say them automatically. That takes a little bit away from the value of saying the pledge

The same thing can happen when we say the Lord's Prayer. We know it so well and we say it so often that sometimes we can be halfway through the prayer before we really start concentrating on what we are saying.

Activity
Say: *Let's say the prayer together, slowly thinking about the meaning of each phrase as we pray it.*

After prayer, distribute the worksheets. Determine in advance how long it should take students working individually to respond in writing to the questions on the worksheet.

On the left side of the sheet are phrases from the Lord's Prayer. After each phrase, there is a question for you to answer about the meaning of the phrase. If you know the answer, write it in the space provided; if not, leave it blank and go on to the next phrase.

(When time is up) *Now please work with another person. Compare and improve each other's answers.*

(When time is up) *Now please move into groups of four and together come up with the best answer you can for each question.*

When time is up, with students still in groups, go through the questions one at a time, randomly selecting groups to offer their answers. Ask for supporting feedback from other groups.

Now that we have devoted some time to really considering the meaning of the words we pray so often, let's end our activity or class with the Lord's Prayer (as described below).

Option
With older students or to shorten this activity, skip ahead immediately and begin by working in groups of four.

Prayer
Divide class in half for prayer, and pray the Lord's Prayer by alternating lines.

The Lord's Prayer Revisited

Our Father | If God is Father to each of us, how should we treat one another? _____

Thy Kingdom come | What would it be like to be ruled by God instead of a human government? _____

give us this day our daily bread | What should we do about those who often go hungry while we are enjoying our daily bread? _____

forgive us our trespasses | What are "trespasses"? Can you give an example? _____

as we forgive those who trespass against us | What should we expect from God if we refuse to forgive others? _____

deliver us from evil | Why don't we just deliver ourselves from evil? _____

23 THE LORD'S PRAYER COLORIZED

Objective
Add personal dimensions to the Lord's Prayer through a fresh and colorful representation of this universally recited prayer. Create a prayer mural.

Catechist background
The Lord's Prayer serves as a point of connection and reflection for all Catholics and all Christians. Around the world, people recite this prayer daily, each in their own language. It is spoken and sung and quietly reverenced in the heart. Even those who lack speech or hearing pray the Lord's Prayer through the medium of sign.

Drawing from imagination, children can assemble their own special vision of the "Our Father." Using crayon/marker and paper, children can share not just how the "Our Father" sounds but how it "looks" to them.

Materials
- ☐ Written or recorded sample of the Lord's Prayer in another language or ASL
- ☐ The entire Lord's Prayer, broken down in phrases with each phrase written on a single strip of paper. (Examples: 1. Our Father who art in heaven; 2. Hallowed be thy name.)
- ☐ Lesson 23 activity worksheets
- ☐ Crayons, markers, masking tape, stapler
- ☐ Large open board space

Lesson Starter
Say: *Today's lesson is about "The Lord's Prayer," so let's begin class by reciting that prayer together.*

(When finished) *Of course you all know that the way we just prayed is not the only way to pray the Lord's Prayer. Here is a sample of how some other people pray this same prayer.* (Play or recite the sample you brought and explain its source.)
We certainly can't improve on the words of Jesus, but we can always work to improve how we understand the words we pray.

Activity.
Say: *I am going to staple a slip of paper to the top of your worksheets. On the paper, there will be one short phrase that is part of the Lord's Prayer.* (Alone or with a partner) *Read the phrase. Think about what you picture in your imagination when you pray these words. Use the rest of the worksheet to create a drawing that represents these words in your mind.*

When all drawings are completed, bring students up in order and attach each labeled drawing, side by side, until the prayer has been completed on available open space.

Option
Follow the same activity plan above, except arrange students in groups of three or four, to work as a team to blend their individual ideas as they work on several consecutive phrases.

Prayer
Invite children to come up around the prayer mural they have created. Have each child recite the words for which he or she is responsible and so complete the prayer.

ACTIVITY SHEET 23

The Lord's Prayer Colorized

24 ARE YOU FOLLOWING JESUS OR SHOWING OFF?

Objective
Discover the difference between "acting" like a Christian and humbly following Jesus.

Catechist background
When we build something, organize something, or even share something, we often expect to receive money, applause, a return favor, or some other form of positive recognition for our effort.

Jesus teaches us that our spiritual acts should not be done to win the praise or approval of others. Our actions are meant to please God, and our rewards will come from God.

Using brief charades and skits, children can explore the difference between fake and real and between hypocrisy and the true faithfulness that Jesus preaches.

Materials
- ☐ 4-5 Charade cards with a simple activity or object for acting out
- ☐ Lesson 24 activity worksheets
- ☐ Random props for worksheet scenes

Lesson starter
Say: *I need three volunteers who like to pretend.* (Select the volunteers, and then say to them:) *Read what is on the card, but don't tell us what is written. When I ask you, please act out what's on your card.*

Those of you watching, please raise a hand when you think you know what the person is acting out. Hint: volunteers will be acting out an object, an animal, or a person doing a job.

Call on each volunteer in turn to act out an age-appropriate object, animal, or occupation. Examples: a lamp, an inchworm, a football cheerleader.

(After the class guesses, say to the volunteers): *Before you sit down, I have a question for each of you.* (Ask if they really *are* the thing they acted out. For example, "So are you really a lamp? An inchworm? A cheerleader?") *Thanks for helping us to see that there is a huge difference between pretending to "be" something and being something for real.*

In the Sermon on the Mount, Jesus encourages prayer, giving alms, and fasting. But Jesus also warns his followers to do these things "for real," not to pretend so that others will be impressed with them or think they are holy.

Activity
On the worksheet there are three passages in which Jesus tells his followers not to *pretend* to be something but rather to actually be it.

Divide the class into groups. Assign each group one of the Bible passages.

Say: *Use the Bible passage and the props you have been given to create a charade or short skit to demonstrate how people (either then or now) often pretend to be holy or righteous.*

Option
Older children may complete the activity above and then reverse the scene so that people are doing holy acts just to honor God.

Prayer
Teach me, Jesus, to pray, give help to others, and sacrifice because such things please you, and not for the praise I might get from other people. Amen.

Are You Following Jesus or Showing Off?

MATTHEW 6:2

When you give alms (charity), do not blow a trumpet before you...in the streets to win praise of others.

• •

MATTHEW 6:5

When you pray, do not...stand and pray...on street corners so that others may see (you).

• •

MATTHEW 6:16

When you fast, do not look gloomy like the hypocrites. They neglect their appearance, so that they may appear to others to be fasting.

25 WHERE DO YOU KEEP YOUR TREASURE?

Objective
Distinguish between earthly treasures that are subject to loss and destruction and heavenly treasure that lasts forever.

Catechist background
A child's concept of "treasure" might include images of pirate's gold or jewel-filled chests they see in movies, or the personal treasures they tuck away in boxes, collection albums, or display cases.

Jesus introduces a third possibility: the treasure we can store up in heaven. By learning to recognize and devote ourselves regularly to storing up treasure in heaven, we make the choice for treasure that lasts forever.

Materials
- ☐ Lesson 25 activity worksheets
- ☐ Catechist's example of material treasure
- ☐ Whiteboard or flip chart and markers
- ☐ Crayons or markers

Lesson starter
Say: *Hands in the air if you like treasures. I brought a few of my personal treasures in to show you today.* (Show sample collections of photos, stamps, fishing lures, old coins, tea cups, or other objects that have special meaning for you.) *What other examples of personal treasures can you think of?* (List on board.)

These are certainly some great treasures. People put a lot of time and effort into getting them. The problem is, these treasure won't last forever. What can happen to these treasures over time? (Draw out student answers, such as "lost," "stolen," or "damaged.")

In the Sermon on the Mount (Matthew 6:19–20), Jesus teaches us to store up treasure in heaven, the kind that will last forever. So how do we get this heavenly treasure? We act in ways that show our love for God and neighbor.

Activity
Divide the class into pairs or small groups.

Say: *On the worksheet, there is a list of six situations you might face at home, at school, with family, friends, or by yourself. After each situation, use the available space to describe what you might say or do to show love for God and neighbor and so store up treasure in heaven.*

Then circle one action that you would be willing to try in the week ahead. Box one action you think the entire class could try. Be ready to discuss and support your suggestions.

Option
Depending on student abilities and interests, assign each student group one situation. Each group would then prepare a skit based on the situation to demonstrate actions that would show love of God and neighbor and store up treasure in heaven. Based on what they saw in the skits, students might then select one approach to store up treasure in heaven during the week ahead.

Prayer
Lord Jesus, help us to spend a little less time on gathering up worldly treasures and a little more time building lasting treasures in heaven through acts of Christian love. Amen.

ACTIVITY SHEET 25

Where Do You Keep Your Treasure?

SITUATIONS	ACTIONS THAT SHOW LOVE OF GOD OR NEIGHBOR (TREASURE)
The first day of school	
Sunday morning	
A friend's birthday party	
When it's time for chores	
At religious education class	
At the mall with friends	

26 WHOM DO YOU SERVE?

Objective
Direct attention, time, and effort to the service of God by serving others.

Catechist background
Young people feel themselves called to many conflicting and demanding pursuits. Schoolwork, sports, clubs, hobbies, family responsibilities, and friendships may all compete to claim available time.

Children may be surprised and challenged by learning that, for Christians, serving God should have priority over all other ventures. A good way to begin serving God regularly can be by serving others.

Materials
- ☐ Lesson 26 activity worksheets
- ☐ Markers

Lesson starter
Say: *Which of these pairs of things do you think would be the most difficult for you to do at the same time?*
- *Do homework and watch television?*
- *Eat crackers and whistle?*
- *Run and read a book?*
- *Talk to a friend on the phone and listen to directions from your parents?*

If appropriate, let volunteers act out some of the conflicts above.

In the Sermon on the Mount, Jesus looks at another pair of activities and tells us that it is impossible to do them at the same time. (Read Mt 6:24.) *He warns us that we can't be fully devoted to God and fully devoted to our own selfish interests at the same time. Sometimes we might forget to serve God because we don't see him. But we do see our siblings, parents, teachers, friends, neighbors, and all of God's creation. When we care for and serve the people and places God has created, we are serving God and not just caring about our own wants.*

Activity
Say: *On the worksheet you will see a column of open hands. Next to the hand you will see the description of someone who can use your help. In the palm of each hand, write words or draw a picture/symbol of what you can hold out to help those persons.*

The bottom hand is reaching out to an open space. In that space, write the name of some person or group you think you can serve this week. In the open hand, write what you will do to serve.

Option
For the last outreach, allow older children to draw names of classmates, write the name of that classmate in the right column, and in the left column write their choice of prayer or service to perform for the chosen student during the week.

Prayer
Almighty Father, help us to keep you in our minds, our hearts, and our actions each day by choosing to serve the needs of others. Amen.

Whom Do You Serve?

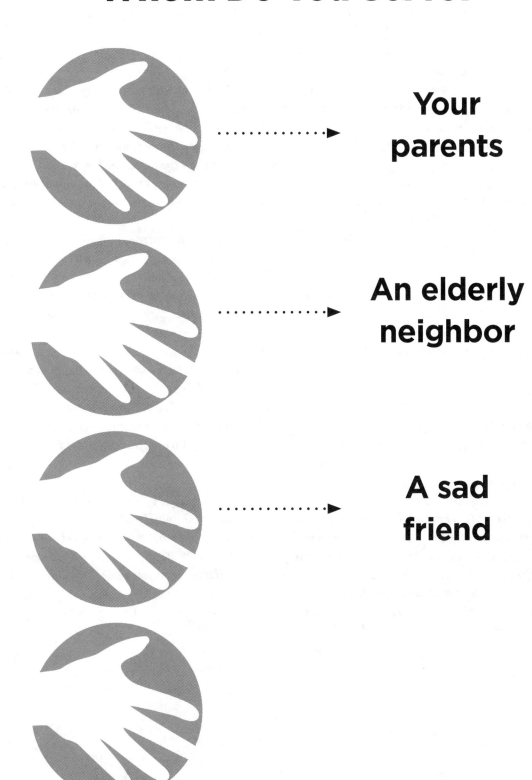

Your parents

An elderly neighbor

A sad friend

IN GOD WE TRUST—OR DO WE?

Objective
Naming what we trust God to provide for us forever.

Catechist background
There is surely no lack of helpful resources in today's world. Without noticing it, children can easily transfer their dependence and their trust from the creator of human beings to what human beings have created.

Examining common resources and reviewing what they can and cannot provide can help children recognize the limitations of man-made products. A comparative exercise can help them to place renewed and enduring trust where it belongs—with God.

Materials
- ☐ Variety of maps, telephone book, grocery store ad pages spread out on a table
- ☐ Lesson 27 activity worksheets
- ☐ Markers

Lesson starter
Before class begins, place familiar resource materials on a display table in a central, highly visible location in the classroom.

Say: *On this table, I have placed a variety of wonderful resources that you and I use everyday. We count on them to help us to do all kinds of things that make our lives more convenient and happy. For example, how can this resource help you?* (Hold up item and call for volunteer answers. Rephrase the question and apply individually to remaining items.) *Even though we rely on resources like these to provide us with services we need, all of these items have definite limits.*

Activity
Say: *On the top half of your worksheet, there are examples of four things in our lives that we trust to behave in a certain way. In each case complete the sentence to tell how you trust the item that is underlined. Then, in the blank that follows, explain how sometimes the item doesn't deliver as you thought it would or should.*

Complete the bottom half of the worksheet by making a list or drawing a picture of the things you know you can always rely on God to provide. Be ready to explain your list or your drawing to your class.

Option
Ask older children to work in pairs or small groups to also produce a prayer in which they give thanks to God for those things that God always provides. Ask students to lead that prayer at each class during the rest of the month.

Prayer
Read Matthew 7:26–30 (according to level of students) and follow with:
We thank you, Father, for all the good things in our lives. Especially we give thanks for those special things that we trust you alone to provide. Amen.

In God We Trust—or Do We?

I TRUST **batteries** to

But sometimes

I TRUST **thermometers** to

But sometimes

I TRUST **stores** to

But sometimes

I TRUST **television news** to

But sometimes

I can always trust God to:

28 THE ANSWER TO OUR PRAYERS

Objective
Center on our own prayer life and believe that God will answer us in his own way, in his own time.

Catechist background
In contrast to electronic devices, God does not respond to us simply because we press a few buttons. Nor is God a remote control that can help us access fun things or exit from situations we find uncomfortable.

In the Sermon on the Mount, Jesus suggests that if we "knock" or "ask" or "seek," we will not go unanswered. Our job is to concentrate on how well we ask, seek, and knock, and leave God to manage the rest.

Materials
- ☐ Picture of an ATM or credit card
- ☐ Lesson 28 activity worksheets

Lesson starter
(As you hold up an ATM card, say:) *Who can tell me what this is? Now, who can tell me how this works?* (Take volunteer responses.) *So basically if I ask the bank for money by pushing a few buttons (and I have money in my bank account), the bank will immediately give me the amount of money I have asked for. If I ask, I will receive.*

Jesus says almost the same thing in the Sermon on the Mount (Matthew 7:7) when he talks to us about prayer. He says: "Ask and it will be given to you; seek and you will find; knock and the door will be opened to you." But the truth is, God does not work like an ATM card. Nor is God a tool that can be programmed to respond the moment we press a button.

Still, when we pray, it's natural to think about the results of our prayer—what we will get and how quickly we will get it. Jesus tells us that we can rely on God to respond to our needs, in his own time and in his own way.

But can God rely on us to pray faithfully?

Activity
Say: *Think about how well you talked with God in prayer last week and then answer the four questions in the box at the top of the worksheet labeled "Week 1."* (Take time to discuss student answers to the first four questions and ideas for how they might pray better. Collect worksheets; hold for redistribution next week.) *During this week when you pray, don't worry about God's answers to your prayer; that's in God's hands. Just concentrate on talking to God: giving thanks and praise and sharing your needs and concerns. Next week, at the beginning of class, I will pass your worksheets back and ask you to write answers to questions in the box for Week 2. Together we can compare the results.*

Option
Older students can continue working on prayer throughout the month by writing in Week 3 and 4 on the worksheet.

Prayer
Generous God, hear our prayers and answer them as we share our needs with you now, silently in our own hearts. Amen.

ACTIVITY SHEET 28

The Answer to Our Prayers

When did I pray?

Week 1: _____

Week 2: _____

What was my favorite way to pray?
(A memorized prayer or my own words)

Week 1 _____

Week 2 _____

Where did I pray?

Week 1 _____

Week 2 _____

Why is it hard to pray sometimes?

Week 1 _____

Week 2 _____

What can I do to pray better?

1. _____

2. _____

3. _____

29 WHAT HOLDS YOUR LIFE TOGETHER?

Objective
Demonstrate the meaning and importance of building your life on a solid faith foundation.

Catechist background
Students help to teach this lesson by building simple model houses. The comparative durability of the houses they construct will help to illustrate the Scripture reading that forms the center of this lesson.

Together, the building and the reading allow you to lead children to discover that faith in Jesus and his teachings is the solid foundation that will help them stand firm and secure in the midst of life's unpredictable challenges.

Materials
- [ ] **Bible**
- [ ] **Lesson 29 activity worksheets**
- [ ] **Collection of building supplies (popsicle sticks, playing cards, building blocks, tinker toys, construction paper, and other materials) that can be used to build small doll-sized houses. (DO NOT distribute glue, clay, or anything that would provide a firm foundation.)**

Lesson starter
Say: *I hope you all have lots of energy today, because I need you to work in pairs, with the materials I am passing out, to build a house—well, actually just a small model house.*

(When houses are finished:) *Now let's read what Jesus had to say about building houses.*

Read Matthew 7:24–27. Discuss the meaning of the passage and then direct students to the worksheet activity.

Activity
Say: *Look at the model house you have built. Draw a rough sketch of what that house looks like at the top of your worksheet. Then respond to the questions you find below your drawing about the materials you used, the foundation on which it rests, how well it would stand up to weather and natural disasters, and what additions might have made it stronger and more weather resistant.*

Now think about your own life and consider the difficulties, hardships, and surprising events that you have to deal with from time to time. Consider what you rely on to get you through difficulties of ordinary living.

When students have completed and discussed worksheet responses, return to and re-read Matthew 7:24–27. Discuss and summarize what is the one true foundation that can hold their lives together and allow them to move from day to day.

Option
Older students work individually to assemble model house and draw worksheet sketch. Then move to a neighbor's desk and use worksheet to evaluate their neighbor's project.

Prayer
Almighty Father, thank you for the beautiful things that surround my life each day—my family, my friends, the things I love to do. Thank you, too, for being the true foundation that holds my life together and on which all my happiness rests. Amen.

ACTIVITY SHEET 29

What Holds Your Life Together?

YOUR HOUSE

What building materials did you use to construct your house?

What is a foundation? Did you have one for your house?

What would happen to a house like the one you built during
A flood?
A hurricane?
An earthquake?

How might the use of glue or cement in the building of your house have made a difference in how well it could stand up to challenges from nature?

YOUR LIFE

With your partner, discuss and list some of the situations and events in daily living that can be hard to manage or that can shake you up and wear you down. What is the true foundation that holds your life together?

30 JOINING THE DISCIPLES

Objective
Outline membership qualifications for those wishing to be true followers of Jesus.

Catechist background
Teams, clubs, and organizations are all part of the social fabric of our lives. The groups we decide to join tell a great deal about how and with whom we want to spend our time and what we value.

When viewed as a type of team or club, the disciples can seem less removed from, and more connected to, our daily life. Children may be surprised, proud, and pleased to discover they share membership in an organization that spans centuries and includes the earliest followers of Jesus.

Materials
- ☐ Whiteboard or flip chart and markers
- ☐ Lesson 30 activity worksheets
- ☐ Crayons or markers
- ☐ A membership card to any organization (real or fabricated)
- ☐ Optional—poster board or banner

Lesson starter
Say: *Those sitting close enough to read what I am holding up, please tell the rest about this card.* (Write the name of the real or imaginary club on the board.) *Help me list on the board the names of teams or clubs to which you or your friends belong.*

Here's the difficult question. When you know the names of the clubs that a person belongs to, what might that tell you about the person? (Using examples provided by children, lead them to see that group memberships tell something about a person's interests, friends, and values.)

We aren't carrying membership cards, but all of us here belong to the same club. Along with people who lived hundreds of years ago, we all belong to a group called "The Disciples," followers of Jesus.

Activity
Say: *Work in pairs or small groups. With your group, use the reverse side of a worksheet to list beliefs that all disciples share.* (Allow all to finish.) *Think of words or slogans you can then write on the team gear you see on the front of the worksheet. Each slogan should only take a few words and tell others a little bit about our team, "The Disciples," and what we believe.*

Option
Enlarge the space available for this activity by replacing the worksheet items with a full size banner or poster board.

Prayer
We give you thanks, Almighty God, for being able to call ourselves "disciples." Help us to always think, speak, and act as true followers of your Son, Jesus. Amen

ACTIVITY SHEET 30

Joining the Disciples

31. THE WORK OF DISCIPLES

Objective
Experience the choices involved in living as true disciples of Jesus.

Catechist background
There is a difference between people who claim to be our friends and those who demonstrate that friendship by their actions.

Jesus captures that recognition when he says: "Not everyone who says to me, 'Lord, Lord,' will enter the kingdom of heaven, but only the one who does the will of my Father in heaven" (Matthew 7:21).

True disciples work each day to follow God's will by obeying his commandments. The choices presented on the worksheet invite children to practice identifying God's will.

Materials
- ☐ Lesson 31 activity worksheets
- ☐ Yellow and blue/black markers or crayons

Lesson starter
Say: *Raise your hand each time a sentence I read describes a true friend.*
- A true friend tells you the truth, even when it's not easy.
- A true friend is usually too busy to listen when you have a problem.
- A true friend tells others you are his friend but sometimes bullies you.
- A true friend always makes room for you on the bus or in the cafeteria.
- A true friend doesn't like you the way you are and is always trying to change you.

We all have our own standards for what makes for a true friend. But most of us would agree that being a true friend means more than just calling yourself a friend; it requires some effort.

In the Sermon on the Mount, Jesus has something similar to say about being a disciple. Listen as I read Matthew 7:21 (as above).

Jesus is telling his followers it's not enough just to call him "Lord." To be real followers, they have to change their way of living and follow the will of God, not their own selfish interests.

Activity
Say: *On the worksheet there are circles enclosing descriptions of specific actions. True disciples of Jesus—those trying to do the will of God the Father—would choose to do some actions but avoid others.*

Practice making the kinds of choices that identify you as a true disciple. Read the description found in each circle. If a true disciple would do what is written in the circle, then use a yellow marker to turn that circle into sunshine. If the action is something real disciples should NOT do, use a blue/black marker to turn the circle into a dark rain cloud.

Be prepared to explain your choices.

Options
Complete the activity above, as is. Then, fill in the two empty circles at the bottom, one with an action disciples would take, and the other with an action they would avoid.

Prayer
Almighty Father, guide our choices each day so that we may be true disciples of Jesus, following your will and not our own. Amen.

ACTIVITY SHEET 31

The Work of Disciples

32. HAVE YOU SEEN ANY DISCIPLES?

Objective
Identify possible disciples of Jesus among the people in your daily life.

Catechist background
Disciples can seem to be remote individuals with whom we have only a very passing acquaintance. What we seldom consider is that disciples are simply those who try to follow Jesus. This means that, in addition to the one we see in the mirror, disciples frequently walk by us without being recognized or acknowledged in any way.

Children can be both surprised and pleased to discover that despite some of life's troubling events, they may very well be in the comforting presence of disciples each and every day.

Materials
☐ Lesson 32 activity worksheets

Lesson starter
Say: *Are there any good investigators in the room?* (Either select a few volunteers or throw it open to the class.) *I'm going to tell you who I'm looking for and you need to tell me what clues might help me in my search.*

I'm looking for—a married person (e.g., wedding ring)
I'm looking for—a cook (e.g., apron)
I'm looking for—a farmer (e.g., overalls, straw hat)
I'm looking for—a police officer (e.g., badge)
I'm looking for—a nurse (e.g., uniform)
I'm looking for—a professor (e.g., briefcase)

Sometimes figuring out a person's identity is not too difficult because we can examine their clothes or appearance. But other times it's not so easy.

Activity
Say: *Disciples of Jesus can be hard to spot; but there are some important telltale clues.*

To find the clues, working in pairs (or small groups), complete the worksheet. Be ready to share your responses with the full class.

Option
Older children may enjoy (non-judgmentally) quizzing one another to see how well they measure up to the clues describing a Christian.

Prayer
Help us, Father, to recognize the many disciples that are part of our community and our world. Let us follow the examples they set and join them as together we try to follow the teaching of your Son, Jesus. Amen.

Have You Seen Any Disciples?

What three prayers might a disciple be able to say?

_____
_____
_____

What kind of people would a disciple tell you were "blessed"?

_____
_____
_____

How would a disciple treat each of these people?

an angry person _____
a sad person _____
a lonely person _____

List three other clues you would look for to find a disciple.

_____
_____
_____

33. MEMOS FROM THE MOUNT

Objective
Take up the work of Jesus' disciples by sharing messages about Christian living from the Sermon on the Mount with other students.

Catechist background
It is certain that some of those listening as Jesus preached the Sermon on the Mount were so moved by what they heard that they shared his message with friends and relatives. While passing along Jesus' words, they increased their own understanding and commitment.

In the same way, students can deepen their knowledge and their faith commitment by taking what they remember from the Sermon and transmitting it to others in a short, personal memo.

Whether catechists decide in advance to have children prepare notes for next year's students, sacrament recipients, classmates, or even family members, the positive results are likely to be the same.

Materials
- ☐ Lesson 33 activity worksheets
- ☐ Fine point markers or pens
- ☐ One stack of self-adhering note paper
- ☐ Bible or copy of Sermon on the Mount
- ☐ Multicolor construction paper
- ☐ Scissors, stapler

Lesson starter
Say: *Today's lesson is going to be about something some of you enjoy—sending notes. I am giving each of you a single memo slip and a pen. Use them to write a memo for yourself listing three things you want to remember to thank God for today. Stick the memo on the inside cover of your book.*

The people who heard Jesus' Sermon on the Mount probably wanted to share some of the words that he spoke. In those times, the best way to pass a message was simply by word of mouth. Today we have simplified the process. If we want to remind someone of something important, quickly and easily, sometimes we use memos.

Activity
Say: *At the top of the worksheet you will find a list of teachings that are taken from the Sermon on the Mount. Select* (1-4, according to student ability) *phrases that you would like to share with* (next year's students or others, as you determine). *Write that phrase in the space provided on the worksheet form. Complete the rest of the message by explaining why you think that teaching is important to remember.*

When memos are complete, direct students to cut them out and staple them to appropriately sized colored construction paper. Memos can then be stored for a board display for next year's class or distributed as you see fit.

Option
Instruct students to design one memo just for themselves as a personal faith reminder. Older students may be directed to use the text of the Sermon on the Mount to discover and use other teachings as appropriate.

Prayer
(Instruct students to open their book covers and take out the memo they wrote at the beginning of class.) *God of Creation, we each come to you now with our own words of thanksgiving for the many good things that have happened to us all.* (Ask students to silently thank God for the things they have written.) *Help us to use the many gifts that you give us each day to love and serve you by loving and serving others, now and forever. Amen.*

ACTIVITY SHEET 33

Memos from the Mount

TEACHINGS FROM THE SERMON ON THE MOUNT

- Be a light to the world
- Be merciful
- Be a peacemaker
- Store your treasure in heaven
- Follow the Golden Rule
- Trust in God
- Don't judge
- True disciples do God's will

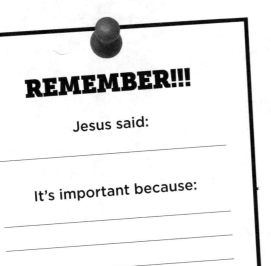

OTHER TITLES IN THIS SERIES

Enriching Faith
Lessons and Activities on What Makes Us Catholic
JANET SCHAEFFLER, OP

In this creative and practical resource, Sr. Janet Schaeffler shows us step by step how to introduce young minds and hearts to the rich treasury of Catholic customs, traditions, rituals and symbols. Each activity includes background for catechists, materials lists, reproducible blackline masters, lesson starters, instructions, prayers, and options to extend the activities.

72 PAGES | $14.95 | 9781627850827

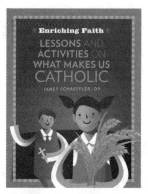

Enriching Faith
Lessons and Activities on the Bible
MARY KATHLEEN GLAVICH, SND

Here are creative ways to introduce biblical lands and cultures, versions of the Bible, biblical reference tools, and techniques for using Scripture as a basis for prayer. Essential topical background, additional teaching ideas, and fun reproducible activity sheets make this a must-have resource.

72 PAGES | $14.95 | 9781627850278

Enriching Faith
Lessons and Activities on Prayer
CATHERINE STEWART

Easy-to-do activities like the bouncing Prayer Ball, Gratitude Grab Bags, and Spoons of Thankfulness can help you teach traditional, spontaneous, creative, and even meditative prayer.

72 PAGES | $14.95 | 9781585959471

Enriching Faith
Prayers and Activities on Service
PATRICIA MATHSON

Help children make Christian service a way of life with this creative collection of outreach projects, hands-on learning experiences, and joyful prayers. Each activity speaks to children's hearts and includes easy instructions, curriculum connections, and more.

72 PAGES | $14.95 | 9781585959372

1-800-321-0411

23RDPUBLICATIONS.COM

TWENTY THIRD PUBLICATIONS